SELECTED POEMS

SELECTED POEMS

John Fowles

Introduced and edited
by Adam Thorpe

FlambardPress

First published in Great Britain in 2012 by Flambard Press
Stable Cottage, East Fourstones, Hexham, Northumberland NE47 5DX
www.flambardpress.co.uk

Typeset by BookType
Cover Design by Gainford Design Associates
Cover photograph © Peter Wiles
Author photograph © Carolyn Djanogly
Printed in Great Britain by Bell & Bain, Glasgow

A CIP catalogue record for this book is available from the British Library.

ISBN: 978-1-906601-35-5 (paperback)
ISBN: 978-1-906601-36-2 (hardback)
ISBN: 978-1-906601-37-9 (e-book)

Flambard Press wishes to thank Arts Council England
for its financial support.

ARTS COUNCIL ENGLAND
LOTTERY FUNDED

Flambard Press is a member of Inpress.

The paper used for this book is FSC accredited.

FSC www.fsc.org
MIX
Paper from responsible sources
FSC® C007785

Editor's Acknowledgements

I am extremely grateful to Sarah Fowles for her patience, generosity and encouragement over the five years it has taken to assemble this book, and for her efforts to find surviving poems and fragments in wayward places. I would also like to thank my daughter Anastasia and my son Sacha for typing out many of the scarcely decipherable poems, and to John Fowles's agent Anthony Sheil of Aitken Alexander Associates for his invaluable support. With thanks also to Peter Lewis (editorial supervision), Will Mackie (production management) and all the team at Flambard Press, who have helped make my work on this book a real pleasure.

Some poems in this collection were previously published in *Poems* by John Fowles (Ecco Press, USA, 1973).

Contents

Introduction

Long ago, in Oxford, I stood in a queue that snaked out of Blackwell's and up Broad Street. We shuffled forward in the October gold, and I was increasingly anxious. It was 1977, I was reading English at Magdalen, and this was the first time I had gone to an author's book-signing. Not only was this author extremely famous, but I had the wrong book. John Fowles was here to sign his new novel, *Daniel Martin*. I was holding *The Magus*, revised version, which had swept me away a few weeks earlier.

In his superb 1986 essay on William Golding, Fowles said of his master that he had become 'Golding', this being 'an entity made entirely of punctuation'. He admits to suffering from the same fate, having become to the public world 'a crude caricature . . . [a] monstrously insufficient surrogate'. As I finally trembled before him in Blackwell's, stammering my excuses, the surrogate was tweaked aside and a roguish smile, a twinkle in the eye, a few kind words through a genial beard took its place as he scribbled a personal dedication.

It would never have occurred to me that John Fowles was shy, that he was much like the characters of his fiction in their adoption of masks for survival purposes or to disguise an existential loneliness – the biggest mask being the writing of fiction itself. Poems were a different matter: in the Foreword to his one collection – published in America in 1973 by the 'very small' Ecco Press – he maintains that 'It is rather difficult to put one's private self into a novel; it is rather difficult to keep it out of a poem'. Novelists, he continues, write novels because of some 'personal inadequacy' or 'fault', arguing that he finds 'the writing of poetry, which I began before I attempted prose, an enormous relief from the constant play-acting of fiction'. (His Foreword is reprinted in full at the end of this book as an Afterword.)

As can be seen by the remarkably long time-span of this Selection[1], his loyalty to poetry never wavered. In the early essay 'I Write Therefore I Am' (1964), Fowles confessed that 'I've always wanted to write (in this order) poems, philosophy, and only then novels'. Fowles was chronologically a poet first and secondly a novelist, but he continued to write poetry (with an apparent hiatus in the 1980s) all his life – even, it has to be said, when he was ill in hospital in his latter years, scribbling biting observations in a large A4 notebook. Readers of his underrated, self-lacerating and often discomfiting *Journals*, written in the waspish Woolfian tradition, will already be aware of the importance to Fowles of both writing and reading poetry.

This has not gone undetected in literary circles. A few years ago, in a review in the *Times Literary Supplement*, the highly respected critic John Greening mentioned in passing 'the neglected poetry of John Fowles', while on the back page of the same issue, reference was made to the Harry Ransome Foundation's purchase of 'thousands of examples of his poetry, only a small proportion of which has been published'. This is a curious situation for a writer of Fowles's continued critical and popular standing. It is explained partly by his success as a writer of fiction, and partly by his own complex dislike of that status: recipient of hundreds of fan letters a year, he was not only a private man (he detested the film world in particular, although a keen cinema-goer) but a modest one. As he puts it in 'Ars Poetica': 'who cares about the patina . . .'

His modesty was not of the false variety: he regarded *The Magus* as 'quite a good novel of adolescence', doubted if *The French Lieutenant's Woman* was 'as original as some people have been kind enough to say', and admitted that *Daniel Martin* 'goes on too much', while confessing (equally mistakenly, in my view) that he was 'not a good

---

[1] *The single poems are set out chronologically, from 'Leigh' (1950) to 'Horror Movie' (1972): the subsequent poems date from the 1990s. The bulk of the poetry, from 'Protect the Word' to 'At Belmont', was written in the 1960s.*

short-story writer' and 'not a good poet' (*Writers Talking*, London 1984).

There are very few writers who would say such things about themselves beyond their immediate circle of family or friends (who usually make the right noises), and in Fowles's case it seems to mirror his remarkable generosity to younger or poorer authors. Having struggled for ten years with *The Magus*, his first fictional attempt, and then written *The Collector*, his first published novel, in a matter of weeks only to see it go on to achieve bestsellerdom, he was acutely aware of how fickle and strange are the ways of both literary creation and critical applause. As he wrote in a reply to an eleven-year-old fan called Alice in 1996: 'Follow and study books, if you must; but there are less pebbly beaches!'

Envy followed in his tracks, of course, not helped by his allergy to the literary establishment – to the hobnobbing, gossip and infighting and the absurd hysteria over prizes. He found his public persona, 'John Fowles', a somewhat alien thing. He was far more concerned with the natural environment, a deep-green ecologist when it was much more fashionable to be a blood-red socialist (although he was a self-confessed Labour supporter of the pre-Blair kind and detested the English class system as much as he did nationalist jingoism). 'The key to my fiction,' he maintained, 'lies in my relationship with nature.' He felt 'intensely close' to the plants and animals in his seaward garden at Lyme Regis, and was perhaps one of the last writers who knew the names of birds, flowers or butterflies as a natural outcome of their upbringing – a poetic knowledge rather than a scientific one. The environmental 'holocaust', as he called it – particularly visible in post-war agribusiness Britain, which he regarded as 'beyond repair' – caused him much anguish at a time when most writers were more worried by social issues. His favourite book, the one that had most influence on him as a boy, was *Bevis*, by the great and somewhat eccentric Victorian naturalist, Richard Jefferies. Fowles's concerns flowered most passionately and completely in *The Tree*, a prose meditation that at times has the lyrical force of poetry.

The fact that Golding and Fowles both started as poets (and in Fowles's case, did not stop) gives to their prose a precise musical quality, an obsession with rhythm, cadence and texture that has been curiously overlooked by critics. Fowles's many remarks on the subject – evident also in his library jottings – show that much of his judgement of this or that work rested on its language, its style, its secret musculature and verbal pulse: thoroughly unfashionable concerns in a literary landscape scorch-earthed by the cruder forces of academic theory. Witness one of the opening sentences of *Daniel Martin*: 'The last of a hanger ran under the eastern ridge of the combe, where it had always been too steep and stony for the plough.'

The prose did not soak up all the poetry. Having read every poem (in mostly manuscript form in their various versions and redrafts) that Fowles ever wrote, I am convinced that he was a fine and serious poet, and that the neglect mentioned by the *TLS* is an unfortunate and wholly unjustified one, whether the readers missing out are scholars of the contemporary novel or the general public.

The abiding theme in his poetry is love, and especially in its classical, 'pagan' form of desire (a kind of enchantment for Fowles – thus his references to Circe). Ovidian regret and longing, added to in the later poems by an awareness of growing old, find their most compelling context in literal Greek settings, where the ancient and the new are mingled and juxtaposed to create both a personal and mythic landscape. Fowles's erotic touch – 'Within ten seconds/I knew I wanted to kiss your eyelids' – is reminiscent of Robert Graves: that sudden involuntary passion echoing the way Fowles first encountered Greece, falling 'hopelessly, overwhelmingly in love' with the wild countryside of the islands . . . and finding his muse quite literally on the slopes of Parnassus, in the form of 'an intensely shy and suspicious young shepherdess'.

Fans of *The Magus* will recognise the quality of this yearning as much as the setting, and Fowles's hypnotic ability to bring the classical universe to life for our own time. The superb 'Apollo Sequence' and 'Mycenae Sequence' are the centrepieces of these 'Greek' poems. The latter demands to be recited aloud: it uses the ancient device of verbal repetition and anaphora to revive the dramatic horror ('doom and hate the demolition/of the heart'), and makes one regret that the collaboration with Peter Hall never included a version of the *Oresteia*.

The 'Apollo Sequence' was written on the island of Spetsai – renamed Phraxos in *The Magus* – and was described by Fowles 'as the ground from which the novel eventually grew'. There were other more literary influences, of course: on that first visit to Greece in 1952 when Fowles began to have, as he put it, 'a real belief in myself as a writer', he read Joyce's *Ulysses*. There was also Alain-Fournier's *Le Grand Meaulnes*, which when Fowles read it as a schoolboy had been 'an experience of such strange force, touching so many secret places [in myself]', that this force re-emerged years later as the compelling mystery of his fictional isle. Other favourite writers not so far mentioned include Voltaire, Flaubert, Cavafy, Norman MacCaig, Flann O'Brien, Stratis Tsirkas, Robinson Jeffers, Basil Bunting, D.H. Lawrence, W.B. Yeats, Garcia Lorca and Paul Valéry.

His shorter, stand-alone lyric poems include many remarkable meditations on nature, inheritance, suffering and desire. 'The Rain Took the Road this Winter' is a moving celebration of his ancestors – anonymous small farmers and peasants about whom he knew very little, 'who never did much bad or good/or got in history's way'. The relaxed diction in this poem seems effortless, yet it is highly crafted – the rhymes never obtrusive. This is Fowles at his best, the quizzical voice combining with the spellbound mystery of the poetic: 'Twice from a window in my heart/I have heard gatherings'. Many of these poems were rescued from oblivion by Sarah Fowles while clearing out her late husband's papers: some are cleanly if faintly typed and have the quality of breath on glass. Others resemble a radio signal dimly made out through a squiggled mass of interference: this was the case for 'Parus Major', a typically Fowlesian glimpse of nature's harsher side, the dead Great Tit reduced to an 'ounce tuft of broken wings' – which nevertheless remains part of what he calls elsewhere, in a brief manuscript note, 'the stupendous nowness of existence – its formidable recurringness'.

There are a host of individual lines that exhibit his familiar control of verbal music ('Your hands range washing down the rock-strewn shore...'), but Fowles's gift for narrative coherence is also present in the verse. 'Crabbing' could have been sunk by its overt ecological dismay, but by concentrating on the perplexed boy, it recovers its poise and still imparts the message. The novelistic grip on character and relationships is brilliantly deployed in 'Chinoiserie', with admirable self-control and a haunting economy acquired through judicious cropping in the manuscript:

I stir my coffee. I do not hear
What the guests are saying.
I am thinking of the ash-trees
Near the castle of Berry Pomeroy.

The slipped mask rarely falls into self-regard. If a footnote suggests that the death-dreaming 'you' of 'At Belmont' is his first wife Elizabeth, the poem, while remaining precisely located, goes on to enact a universal 'terror' in the unused loft's suspenseful darkness. And sometimes, when he speaks for instance of 'a dark new steel feudality' clouding the land, Fowles seems to update Blake in the anticipation of our own calamitous lack of care for both nature and people.

What of the poems not included in this Selection? They tend, in my view, to be let down (rather than enhanced) by Fowles's novel-writing half, usually in the form of a pair of prosaic buffers in the last verse, the firm closure of a couplet. This is always a danger for the poet-novelist: that exposition and the sheer range of human ordinariness covered by fiction may pin the poem's wings, whatever the diction's lyrical register. Similarly, I have excluded verse that seemed fatally damaged by a certain acidic bitterness against the outside world, usually in the form of satire – what he called his 'cranky black rhinoceros' side. The scrawled, semi-legible 'Posh Hospital Poems' were an exception: embittered, certainly, but with a sense of compassion and a gallows humour that is almost heroic, capturing that medical-warded state of being, that forced idleness that lets the mind wander semi-coherently between memory, daily survival and thoughts of the end: 'It is absurd, the hedging day on day, to funk the brink/One cannot cross.'

Translation was very important for Fowles, who studied French at Oxford; he reckoned the first work of his that could be called 'original' was, paradoxically, 'a translation of a well-known French poem'. His translation of Molière's *Dom Juan* was produced by the National Theatre in 1981; sadly, he never finished the script, likewise commissioned by Peter Hall, of *Le Grand Meaulnes.* The translations and versions drawn from, among others, Aristophanes, Martial, Catullus, La Fontaine and Li Po deserve to see the light of day: most are doing so for the first time. He took this difficult task extremely seriously, and was proficient in Latin as well as French. From the eighth-century *Man'yoshu*, Japan's oldest poetry compilation and the most revered, he conjures exquisitely tempered reflections which count among his finest achievements in verse.

Fowles is, like Dickens, that very rare phenomenon of a deeply literary author becoming wealthy and famous entirely through his works. Late in his life, as a private jotting in the *Diaries* of Kenneth Tynan, Fowles wrote: 'I didn't like this book at all. Knowing everyone means in the end you know no-one.'

Perhaps blinking confusedly in his own celebrity, he chose a different path, not only sticking to his beloved Lyme Regis but becoming its little museum's curator, a celebrator of the local, the provincial, the fragile bric-à-brac of ordinariness – and diving into the woods where he was self-confessedly happiest, because trees have no words.

Yet the advantage of poetry over prose fiction, he reckoned, is that the reader 'shall know the writer better at the end of it'. Although those fictional masks have been removed, something of the mystery of an individual creator, as well as of life's nowness – so precious to Fowles – remains intact. In a rueful interview conducted by his friend Dianne Vipond in 1995, Fowles admits, 'I wish I could have been an excellent poet.' I hope the reader agrees that the following pages remove the conditional tense from that wish.

Pasted into a copy of Paul Valéry's *Eupalinos* (bought with Fowles's very first earnings as a young English tutor in Poitiers in 1951), is the following typewritten note: '. . . *this 16.2.96. stuck in the invalid chair in my bedroom here at Belmont. I dream, in my dropsy, of Athikté; lead thinking thistledown.*' The succinct and effortless beauty of that final sentence is remarkable: here is the leaden body in counterpoint with the weightless yet fertile imagination symbolised by Athikté, the healing dancer in Valéry's dialogue *L'Âme et la Danse*. And here is the ailing, elderly writer looking back on his youth – still writing, still letting that mysterious breeze take the seeds to fall where they will.

Adam Thorpe

Monoblet, France
April 2012

Ars Poetica

spending too much time on
the patina; altogether too much
time on the patina

who cares about the patina

altogether too much time
on matters thought to matter

as if you judged it by patina and catalogue title,
by what's said about it
in the catalogue

when it's what it says
about him: there, this
was what he was

this shape, this *thing*

they should be like the
little daily things kept
in Doctor Johnson's house:
his tea-bowl, stick, reading stand

like a map of your garden
like a visit to you

so when you're dead and
they read your collected
they'll say:
I see how he was

An Old Draft

The poem one wrote,
When all seemed well.

This alienation from what one was
Or it seems one was.
Terrible the poem,
The words assembled by some stranger,
The one less sure of words,
Less clear in purpose, less possessed
Than even the least had right to be;
Who tried by trying,
Chased his own tail,

And so to this: the shards,
The fallen house of tat-edged cards,
The terrible unshifting eyes;
The eyes of the tyrant king
Who sees nothing, nothing, in each hope,
And nothing in each past but lies.

APOLLO

A Sequence of Greek Poems

These poems are some of those I wrote when I lived on the island of Spetsai, which became 'Phraxos' (the 'fenced' island) in The Magus. *They date mainly from 1951–52, and I have included them here because, together with the sense of loss I felt when various circumstances obliged me to put myself in permanent exile from Greece, they were the ground from which the novel eventually grew. The poem called 'Apollo' was especially important in this context. Spetsai had (I am afraid universal tourism has made the past tense necessary) natural mysteries far deeper than the artificial ones that I eventually put in my fiction. I think I know why the ancient Greeks gave the place such a wide berth. [John Fowles]*

Islanders

they look to sea and wait
these carved immobile men
beneath the cool catalpas
these aged women pausing
by the polished upward steps
they look to sea and wait
for what they cannot say

he waits
for what he cannot say
this canvas seaward boy
by the corner of my house

never the ship that comes
never a bird never a cloud
what it is they cannot say
whether good luck or unkind fate
but look to sea and wait

at first I laughed but now
I look to sea and wait
for what I cannot say:
but look to sea and wait

The Aegean Sadness

Sun upon sun distils the land
Over the pulsing, cobalt sea;
Sun upon sun and endless sun,
Scent of wild resin, cicada-song.

Olives and wine and small fried fish,
Aeon-dark islanders lost in shade;
Day after day we sit on the terrace,
Over the waves and unknown lives.

So strangely sad, this heat and sun.
Is this why they left to sail for Troy?
To make the same sadness seem complete –
To kill Astyanax and call it joy?

Villagers

these villagers
who watch my mouth
emergence of
each foreign sound

as if it were
some Pythian bouche
some dawn that utters
strange new birds

now make me silent:
they want too much
I want too little
with my words

Anadyomene

This octopus: I watch it walk,
The suckered arms of Aphrodite
Over the creviced lawn of weeds,
Fluid, full, in my same flux.

I strike: hoist the tall trident.
Her dying arms obscure the sun.
Love is dead, now peace is won.
I turn: and there they stand,

The triad greater than the gods,
Socket-eyed and stony-limbed,
Basalt-black on the sunlit shore
And waiting to enact the law.

At a Village Between

before these faces
where the ribs of the children stare like strakes
where the men on the doorsteps have no words
where the women in black with hollow cheeks
stare at their ikons
no longer asking but still believing

and before those faces
lost in their limousines
masks of gold that accelerate through

the rage of Orestes is
how in that swirl of dust not choose

Unasked

here on his terrace our charming host
Mr Plutopoulos the impeccably rich
poised like his palace cool and
white in the pale eucalyptus

he had his Cadillacs
his pink Picassos and his Braques
his cocktail bars his planes his yachts
his men his softened ministers
his well-connected breeding wife
and they say his latest mistress
is la Loren to the life
lost in a pool of sleek brown men

with dapper gestures cast in gold
lost in a dusk of perfumed women
the cream of the embassies Kolonaki
I stand and observe

gold gold I drown in gold
he comes I hear demotic French
iced drinks Matisse we make
the politest cultured pair

with all the usual lack of will
I do not ask what I should ask
under this golden death of sky
I do not ask our charming host
the anglophile the golden smile
how he dare presume
there is a hovel in the world
where those who starve are not his victims

Aboulia

what are we doing here
wasting time by the ochre road
under the pepper-trees
swilling cheap wine

the Greeks in white shirts
the Greeks in white shirts
what are we doing here
wasting time until it hurts

waiting and boozing
at frantic noon
nobody knows when night will come
but thinkers think it could be soon

the lisp the press the weave
and stress the old Greek hive
the gestures phonemes facial fuss
and it is nothing at all to us

here we sit like Xerxes
the flower defeated
dislocate couplets
old rhymes repeated

barbarians *Inglesoi* men of the north
only half living in all this light:
watching the bus we should have caught
draw for eternity out of our sight

Shepherd

at the stone glade-end
he stands from the firs
and offers greetings
old bread
warm milk
a cheese

takes my hand and cigarette
we talk
whether there will be war
what I do in life
how long it takes to fly to London
and the sea of bells

each minute he whistles
soft searching whistles
between question and answer
bells and whistles

once he worked in Athens but
came back rare one to the mountain
Parnassus racked with wolves and cold

Athens was good but lacked one thing:
a silence in which a man could sing

Tourists at the Erechtheion

Mounting the famous marble hill,
The people come, the people stand
And stare; and then consult their guides,
But later stare again, since guides
Have never helped one here.

They see the sisters in the sun,
They try to tease their meanings out.
The too hermetic smiles upset:
What they know we do not know
Must be the joke they smirk about.

The endless tourists photograph,
Record each smile, then turn away
With trite awed faces, solemn looks:
Too humourless, too pale, too small
To grasp the sisters' point at all.

Straggling back to their plush hotels,
The same old blind Boeotian herd –
Some Paul should stop them, shout the truth.
No god can have a serious face:
It is the smile that is the Word.

Byzantium

Purples on purples, faecal browns,
Neurotic greens and wombing blacks,
Crusted walls and cancerous cells:
And I stand in the narthex hating
Byzantium, inward Byzantium,
These vile Greek churches staling
Their landscapes like poisonous fungi,
Clusters of foul mycotic caps,
Enshriners of the worst of night.

I know Byzantium: Byzantium
Is anything that tortures light.

The Noble Youth of Athens

I like best the one
who speaks no English word
but yes
yet talks and talks

who always grins
and limps more quick
more eagerly
than any client walks

strangely pure
the bright-faced boys
like wild spring buds
the bright-faced pimps

A Kind of Philhellene

Hearing them talk, the slick expatriates:
The essence of Greece, and all that jazz –
Lines from Seferis, Ghika's latest, what
Miller's Katsimbalis said last week.

Not one has walked in the real land,
Where any chance-met peasant's mouth
Can give you Greece to its deepest core
And from the beginning to the end.

Who art thou?
Where from?
Where to?
And for thy bread, what dost thou do?

All you who come to 'write' or 'paint' –
God help you if you smile at this
And find those questions merely quaint.

It Is a Lie

Riesis the small,
The brown, the simian man
With indelible eyes,
He is not dead.

With the hoopoe's laugh.
I say he is not dead,
I see him still
By the dazzling wall.

He hides in these leaves,
I hear him.
These lilac leaves.
Among these leaves.

Death to the rumours
He died in Athens;
Of cancer, midnight,
Under morphine.

Death to them, death.
His bright brown laughter
Breeds green leaves.
See, it is spring again.

Tomorrow all those
Who have stood
At my side
Shall dance.

The lilac will bring
White cones of light,
And nightingales creep
In the laurel-rose.

Apollo

the stones the pines
the shadow of pines
on the singing stones

gurgle of stones
turned in the sun
by the silent water

the water like glass
pale glass
the sun on the water
the stones in the water
the pines and the stones

the salt stones singing
and the sea singing
and the pines and the sun
singing

a yellow sea-poppy
sun and shingle
sea and silence

shrike screams
I come

THE MYCENAE SEQUENCE

The personal background to the sequence is as follows: in the high summer of 1952 I visited Mycenae. The only person I saw all day was a shepherd. Like every Greek July day it was one of brilliant sun, but the enormous counterweight and desolation of Mycenae have to be experienced to be believed. Some conjunction of myth, of Aeschylus, of landscape, of massive entrapping architecture, hangs like a cloud over the place. Every visitor there has felt it; and perhaps because I was alone, and in more senses than one, I felt it overpoweringly that day in 1952. Near midnight, as a sort of test, to prove to myself that I was not afraid of the atmosphere of Mycenae, I left the inn where I was staying, walked back up to the ruins and there forced myself to go into the most sinister of the beehive tombs (the Treasury of Atreus) and to sit for half an hour in the inner room. Of course nothing supernatural happened, but the experience remains a very powerful one in my memory. I don't know what it meant, or means; but I have always felt since in some sense possessed by Mycenae. At the time I felt I had conquered the place; but that was Anglo-Saxon stupidity.

When I came out of the tomb I went to the citadel and sat on top of a wall, in brilliant moonlight. While I was there a scops owl flew and perched on the wall only a few yards away; a little later a vixen came and stood in the road below me; this second incident, the bird, the animal, and myself, in the moonlight, in a kind of mysterious union, has also remained vividly and actively in my memory. The vixen finally disappeared down the so-called tomb of Clytemnestra; a villager told me the next morning that it had its earth there.

In the year following this visit I found myself in the Oresteia situation. There cannot be any connection between my visit to Mycenae and the events that occurred in my private life the next year. I had not even heard of the other two protagonists at the time of that visit; yet I feel there was something at Mycenae for me to understand; something terrible, and that because I could not see it, or was afraid to see it, then I had no chance of dodging the role I was later to play. I had to enter the situation; to return to Mycenae and live there evermore.

Plainly, I have departed very far from the Oresteia. As regards the chorus: it seems to me that the attitude I explicitly take towards them is implicit in Aeschylus. I see my chorus as a group of the elderly 'educated' polloi; *awled hollow, made mirrors, by their belief that to observe and to record accurately is all that life requires of human beings. Most scientists seem, whatever they say, to hold to this belief; it is also of course the immemorial attitude of the true* polloi, *the great masses. Strange allies, the scientists and the masses; but there it is.*

Equally plain, I hope, is one secondary intention: to defend not adultery, but certain humans in certain situations. [John Fowles]

Choros

this is the everwounded world
we call Mycenae this the
cutting of black gates into earth
and blood the clocks will never staunch

these are the terraces painted shards
these the stained ombres on the wall
here is the lions' endless waiting
blood upon blood roar and shrieking

these are the gods in the golden masks
watching each footstep from the sky
implacable hazard rules this world
the counters never shall know why

these are the seeds of love in lust
and the seeds of death and the cry
in the night and the axe are these
and this the king on the gypsum floor

and this black slot in the ochre earth
the central tomb the uninterable past
that will not die; still in the marble
sits the old watchman's lizard eye

and it is now the lions now the door
the hour and now the hate begins
again again the black bloods blend
the wounds are made and without end

mysterious marriage at Mycenae
Agamemnon sails each day
poor Clytemnestra turns again
Aegisthos cannot walk away

it is now it is now there is
no past there are no dead
this hill is gashed eternity
it bleeds it bleeds it never bled

Cassandra

the mirrors come
the time is ripe

the dead live again
the time is ripe

hands from the shadow
the time is ripe

the flaming mouth
the time is ripe

vixen and owl
the time is ripe

the lions stir
the time is ripe

now the black apex
time is ripe

so reap

Aegisthos

I come in hazard to these heavy hills
year twenty-eight of missing life
and all I see is dust; I know
reality is grist for death

I am this shadow on the lonely road
no flesh for love

I stand aloof in the busy street
and what I hate instructs each crowd

I lie awake through hollow nights
counting the long hours through to dawn
which comes
and then I turn and curse the sun

stony paths I ride down
lead to meetings meaning nothing
to long days desert-long with words
words words abuse of the words
and night the ineluctable; the
naked limbs the clonic sweat
the hour on white hour of open eyes

I know that hidden owl that cries
day is the wrong proposition
appropriate masks the amassing of facts
kingdom of counters the ages' men

I do not hold the statesmen dear
the frightened spenders of our blood
where others know, I am not sure;
would sooner read a dead man's book
than go to war

dust casing dust; and I am dust
a little too clear
I am Aegisthos knower that
nothing is, except the case;
where you who cross my path hold hope
I hold despair; and even death
reads nothing nothing in my face

Choros

he believes in a general unbelief
and that is bad

the attention to self
is also bad

what is established disestablishes
his heart

no heart no faith no love if
we had pity but we have no pity

and the next is not a human being
but a grand historic role

he rules he makes decisions he respects
the law we like him

if we had hands but we have no hands
we have only voices

we are neither living nor dead
but a cloud of words

we have highly placed friends gods
in the know

they have told us who comes
and whom he will meet

she is watching the causeway the gate
beware watching wives

these two their misfortune is this
they are not like us

we shall give them the traditional advice
but they will not hear it

we know this will happen; the law
is what has happened before

Agamemnon

the tortured hounds
bay at their leash-chains challenge day
and countless havoc cries the horn

we of the booming bronze tracheae
great Agamemnon of the red domaine
black weapon of the unworked will
ride with our cavalcade of kings
over the cowed domestic plain

here in a hut a blind man counts
over the eagles the vultures wheel

terrified footsteps down the hillside
voices of torment echoing woods
over the meadows of poppies in sun
and we are the galloping noon
of blood; here
at the kill we pause and stand
downshadowed dagger looming hood;
because of what we are and must
we thrust
home and home drive ever home
we the harrow scything hook
maker of harvests future seed;
to kill is always a fertile deed

with flaccid hands we canter back
over the silent plain at dusk
black waves of red huntsmen
that break the dry stubble

Clytemnestra

poppies
poppies
I think of nothing picking poppies

the red silk
stiff corn
wind in the papery

I am these small dark hands
snapping the delicate hairy stems
I am and I am
this sea of hot blue solstice air
the high-slit circles of the swifts
the insects
murmur
plants and sun

naked

sky
and warm airs these
limbs the earth loves
me flowers burn
to touch

standing here
standing here
poppied shoulders
in the uncut corn

thought sinks years
whirl
to be
to be

to be crushed back in it
crushed to the hot dry earth in it
trampled straw and burring ears
the bed of it beaten under my back
pressed down down in it the torture
of the passion rage crushed crushed
the swathes
and then receive

dark speck in the valley
this sudden wind
why why

I am a goddess in a shower of blood
red twists of spiralled petals rise
corn rustles round my darkening thighs
scream of the swifts
who comes who comes
who makes me
stream of the golden arms and hair
immortal in ascending wind

Choros

we have had dealings with them
mostly by flight of birds
by dreams
by xoana fallen in our fields
augurs have helped us and men of science
so we know

even though we have not seen them
we know

they are envious very envious
they cannot move
we can
they cannot begin and end
we can
they cannot have sex
we can
they cannot choose
we can
our reality is varied and theirs
is monotonous
we are here to amuse them

we are racked between poles
we float we drift we react
we trace meaningless patterns insects
on water pause and skate pause
and skate
and it is all to give the time
to hate

so obey and respect them
they are greater than us
stand still it is safest
concealed in shadows

movement betrays
the lightning likes the greenest sap
stand still stand still
or move
and one day walk into their trap

Aegisthos

here from the high forbidden room
slatted shadows caged in laws
I see you on your burning roof
lie in the arms of April sun

form and untouchable loveliness
light flows between us

and you go to the parapet
look down on green gardens
shadowy birds
children invisible under the branches

now raise your long arms to the sun
your rich hair falls
impulse of hands
and you are naked:
I watch I watch tormented I watch
I am the air that lips your skin
your naked arms your naked legs
and you lie and you move
thigh and ankle pointed breast
you sit you comb hair
touch skin view hands
set arms in positions sculpt bright air

you walk and you dance and you walk
dancing

arms upraised
slender dark armpits
and twisting up your dark red hair

and now the tremor
you turn in fear I touch the wall
earth tilts my eyes and you together
nothing nothing a moment's tremor
two flames' contortion in the sun
twisting twisting dark red hair

and in one moment
all the destined damage done

Agamemnon

she waits she waits we come her king
we Agamemnon now who reel and belch
quickvoider killer phallic man
bullshadow in the untorched door
and strip her from her golden couch
to have her forced-legs on the floor

and when we snore among our fumes
how should we know she lies
and waits and in her seething waiting
wheels

Aegisthos and Clytemnestra

so in the white labyrinth
the complex hill of hissing voices
we meet at last
the longsought eyes

how many years
searching looking
seeing the other eyes
see in vain
question and question
no response

mask and machinery
never this
the confrontation of the eyes
and this

the fuse and the firegale
vortex/cosmos
fire on fire

we fall
we fall
through uttermost ends
still unbegun
one and two now
two now
in this mystic one

Choros

here we are tracing the course of events
on the roadside sand

sooner or later an event will occur
forming the hypotenuse so and
Agamemnon an angle without an outlet
a walled-in window
a room that never was
no light any more
the axe will fall

and observe
the angles of the hypotenuse
are walled in also
inescapable prison
destiny
a triangle is one
encloses

consider therefore our wisdom
when we make it our rule
bearing in mind that events cause angles
never to cause events
but to hear of events
to read of events
to observe events
to stand at events and surround events
to collect events
but never repeat never to cause events
to keep the arms folded
is the official pose

we regret this small wind
that obscures the diagram
please excuse us
sand is useless

Agamemnon

under the keel the calm sea sings
and here
high in the prow we preen prink
in our glittering golden armour

now sing the old legends
and arms of other men's eager wives
we
with a lightness in our hearts
only the mountains under melting show
the sailed towards
can with their upthrust summits tell

here on our deck of driven time
by arrogant mast and slanting plank
we the revived
live our rich onwardness

kings and comrades chthonic men:
what else is our any coming war
but pretext for the vital voyage
whose we stand
the black the bronzed
all time's mechanics men of arms
high in each eye of each onward prow
each wild unknown tomorrow
taut in each brilliant now

Clytemnestra

is it in the unleashed look
or in the treacherous air
in what unwise old women say
or precognition of the yet unwritten book

but our oblique and unlanced eyes
and then our tense untouching hands
our silences
and now our silence by the shore

and how one cannot turn
one cannot turn
from the web the maze
the minotaur
the painted footsteps on the floor

and how in the womb
one cannot choose
one cannot turn;
the swift-repeated pattern
of the automatic loom

and we mysteries in mysteries
blind woods of nightingales
weeping whole epochs in ten wild notes

but take these flowers
now
take these flowers
and say no word

Aegisthos

on a day of endless rain
of endless rain

of swelling streams
of splitting seeds
migrating birds:
your saffron mouth

and the rain:
your saffron mouth

dawn to dusk
the endless rain
the rain the rain
the alley rain:
your saffron mouth

and in the humid night
you came naked
from the endless rain
stood at the door
beyond the rain:
your saffron mouth

warm wanton tongue
in saffron mouth

your sun and saffron
wanted wanton
saffron mouth

your saffron mouth
and still the rain

Aegisthos

waking that dawn
seeing you stand in the quiet light
the amber of the unborn sun

watching a thing
I could not see
below the eastern window's sill

standing naked

caught in a moment of absent combing
your summer hands upon your hair

silently stood

continued to comb then saw my eyes
my watching eyes

and we watched
across the flooded dawn-grey room
across the sound of singing birds
arrested combing woken sleep;
watched our same mysterious eyes
after a night of all-changing love

Clytemnestra

what I led you to
was never this;
somewhere inside the labyrinth
the way was lost

here at the hub
and interlocked
we looked for death;
doom and hate the demolition
of the heart in orgies guilt
to drain adulterous blood

but here the only horn
is silence; we turn
Aegisthos
not knowing how to say
in a moment of strangeness
multiple death
that this is love
and more

not lust not lust
but love and more
this is the minotaur
black-white eudaemon
that we should meet
spring across reason water blood
should fuse together in our night
and now

alone
but one
and one in that one
in otherwise inhuman light

Choros

there they are
entering the trees
let us surround the trees
let us creep between the trees
let us find an observation post
let us see if it is sex
likely to finish soon
or the vile iniquity of love

it is love the forbidden act
tell the wind
see that it gets to the ears of authority
you know who
say
love has been perpetrated

look at them them look at them
coupling there in that ditch of flowers

there there surround them
he has her among the flowers again
and the lark sings over them
they think they are gods
this cannot be

go wind and do your duty

Clytemnestra

I wake again
the dream again was poppies
in my husband's hair

then doomed we lie;
you sleep I wait
for the watchman's broken cry
the chaos in the common throat

Agamemnon Agamemnon
age upon age of relentless return
implacable setting of cause on cause
implacable movement of blind machinery
conjunctions of dice on inlaid boards
irrefrangible onward deathward trance
down the long cutting and to the door

what is this irrevocable
this road of life
these lynx-eyes in the antique frieze
this destiny I never was

you
who came to me
stood in the shimmering August wind
speaking songs and secret flowers
to turn anonymous and uncut tombs
to public myths notorious crimes;
and now

the palace sleeps;
and yet
what peace
what strange togetherness of peace

Leigh

Winter,
the wild wind wounds the trees.

Childhood,
that endless wounded whining
in the iron outside pipes.

Downstairs
the wireless droned immortally
important Sunday hymns.

*

Between the bitter blackthorn
and the unflowered dyke
the tide-ebb runs.

Voiceless, wingless,
the thousands pass;
from home to city

from city home.
Seaward the driftwood.
Listless tide.

Deathward, seaward,
between the bitter blackthorn
and the unflowered dyke.

Failed

Not sit as in a cinema,
not see on the treacherous screen
two-dimensional women's breasts
and all that we might have been.

Not sit in a cinema all my life,
finding no exit, no end
to obscurity.

Not on my way home
to the house like every other house,
the street like every other street,
the shabby room and backstreet silence.
Not home to the silence.

Finding no exit.
Being even afraid of death.

Epiphenomenon

Strange moments at the seismograph
When imperceptibly the needle shakes:
It is like the echo of an echo
Of a closing door in an empty house,
Or the distant crack of unseen ice
Deep in the glacier's shifty core.
What you become is suddenly
Beyond the weak science of your growth.

Enrolment

Enrolment is our enemy;
Enrolment taking us unaware
Like upturned crabs.

Always the terrible tribe or club,
Always the woad or emblazoned tie;
There is even a Club des Sans-Club.

Our endless desire to belong;
The long stampede, the intershock
Of herds and hordes. Ah, if

We could only respect our selves,
Not always sell mind for membership.
Be pioneers, and hew our own good wood.

Yes, be pioneers, be real men,
Leave this primitive party age
And enter the era of memberlessness.

One Can Allocate Children

One can allocate children,
And we are all children,
To one of two great groups.

Those to whom to return home
Is to rediscover sanctuary,
And those to whom home is
Spent or unspent agony.

But sympathy is out of place.
It would be difficult to tell
Which group knows more of hell.

Umbrae

In the small quantum of each leaf
Each quick long summer falls.
The hurtling pavement has that speed
You race now as you read.

I am this shadow on the leaves,
The leaves these shadows on my head.
Shadow and shadow make up life
And the endless light means I am dead.

The Secret

you cannot tell it to the sky
and the trees do not want it:
the machine does not want it
and men are men

shout and shout it where you want
and again and again and again:
you might as well speak Greek to stones
as this to other men

so shout it in their stupid faces
or dress it up in art:
but nobody wants what you know
inside your deepest heart

nobody wants your secret:
on winter nights it sometimes seems
we might as well be dead
as live like this and keep it

A Definition

The highwayman never hangs;
Always, just before the end,
A cry – a cry in the crowd,
And the rope hangs empty sky.

But when the crippled king
Appears, self-damned, on high,
No cry. No cry in the crowd,
But bleeding eye and bleeding eye.

The highwayman canters away,
His resurrection teases.
The unhanged god's hermetic smile:
A fantasy always pleases.

But the human art is the awe
Of the unrepeatable act,
The absolute death of dreams;
What is, and not what seems.

Au Clair de Lune

one night as they lay sleepless
with the moon across their bed
since you've been away I've
slept with another man she said

and he: I am that alien man;
the one you loved who went away
fell from the edge of the world one day
and can be safely counted dead

moonlit silence froze between them
they lay there stiffly side by side
after a while she turned her back
and foetally bent her knees and cried

one night as they lay sleepless
with the moon across their bed
they came to this they came to this
they loved the each other that was dead

Sibilus Aurae Levis

the wind
the swelling net
the small damp air in the idle net

fish too small for the silent mesh
mysterious wind that cannot be

with a smell of rain
but there is no rain

with the smell of firs
wet firs
but there are no firs

some other wind
on this banal and windless landing

is that it
is now a lie

Chinoiserie

The steam rises from my urine.
The guests talk in the bedroom.
I am very close, and very far.

I stir my coffee. I do not hear
What the guests are saying.
I am thinking of the ash-trees
Near the castle of Berry Pomeroy.

They say the obvious things.
We make the obvious replies.
Why, is not clear.

I listen for the room's voice.
It speaks a peasant word
For silence. No one hears.

The guests praise recent music.
I would much prefer
The wind in the seven pines.

Protect the Word

Protect the word,
Protect and cherish the word,
Cherish and preserve.

The word has many enemies;
Things as they are
Are not of help.

Music-lovers, lovers of art,
Empty shells, mere seeing eyes,
Are not of help.

At the beginning was the word,
Before the image or the sound.
In chaos, order is its heart,

In order freedom is its soul.
It is the art in which to feel
Is not enough, and yet in which

The best are not the most skilled.
There seemed many great auks
Till the last one was killed.

Mirage

Champagne, Chanel and chandeliers,
That capital, that capital free life,
The dream we are all three sisters to,
That febrile salon of the great,

How grand until today is reached.
For even at the public heart of things
Today is provinces, is dialects, is dead
Ubique saying again what Tchekov said of

Ladies in turn-of-the-century gowns,
Lost lilac faces against the cold window,
Youth reduced to a fusty anaphora,
Farewells on platforms by empty tracks.

I see our hated and familiar nows
Meet to discuss and yearn and plan
And breed that desert-making heresy
That happiness is having what one lacks.

Di multa neglecti dederunt mala

Why let the metaphor 'the heart' still live,
When words are tools to be used with skill,
Not love? When charity is fixed, a
Sum slick Christians are advised to give?

When money-minds and mass-ambitions
Bruise down the ever-narrowing street,
When taking and lying mean success
And the sensitive are nicknamed beat?

When few care for 'the heart' any more.
For the small proleptic heart – when all
Is technique, the latest vogue, the look
Of the thing, and even that in art?

When a dark new steel feudality
Now clouds the souring land;
When if Demeter came again
We could not even see her hand.

The title is taken from Horace's Odes, book 3, poem 6: 'The gods neglected gave many bad things.' [Editor]

Never to Be

alone in the grove of silent eyes
the flicker gloom of the lying screen
I saw last night a one not any other
waiting for an unknown lover

and later I saw her in a café
wearing her loneliness like a scent
red-haired grey-eyed sweetsour nineteen
o God what pleasures might have been

if I had come ten years ago
to this same hour and this same place
alone and stood and smiled and she
like Io with the waiting face

Between the Arclights

Walking down Liverpool Road, 2 December 1961

Between the arclights
lumina nocte gemina teguntur
there is a point
where the shadow goes
only the ghost of the shadow
split
two ghosts

with two petty ghosts
I walk
and at the brightest point
sharp
black lightning
Rorschach makes sense
my jetblack flame my moving death my end
is:
I-shall-die is
spilt Indian ink electric
on the neutral pavement

the walker
the shadow
and who is light

The second line in Latin is from Catullus LI:
'Twin nights cover my eyes.' [Editor]

The Experience

You go down the right turnings
just as it says in the guide,
and it isn't there.

You turn up at the right room
at the right time,
in the right month and moonlight;
and it isn't there.

You discover the right grove,
you stand about on damp leaves.
A man on a tractor passes
and thinks you are mad.

You have the paper and the time,
you have the lot,
and nothing comes.

And it comes
at the start of a busy day
as you shave in a hurry,
cog with no time.

The wind. And you stand,
blinded till you are not blind.

Within Ten Seconds

Within ten seconds
I knew I wanted to kiss your eyelids.
This is why I kept staring
Past you, as if to a cold horizon.
You were not boring me, as you thought.
I was looking to where you stood
Smelling of rain, with naked breasts.
Naked, defenceless, needing defence.
It was not as you thought,
You were piqued and moved away.
I was the one who by silence,
Staring, no move, moved away.

Where pine trees touch water.
I am
Men who tie themselves to masts.
You are
Sirens with delicate eyelids.
Penelope is white with lust.
Molpe, the deck has tears
And the rock has tears.
Even the sun has molten tears.

Meeting, never to meet again.

By the Appian Way

A white wind blows from the distant sea
And the Alban hills are lost in heat.
We march, you remember, we march
The straight black road and the broken tombs,
Then sit on this mound in the shade of pines
And see its straightness,
Its arrogant endless Roman straightness.

And the broken tombs.

The sadness is there is no sadness.
Only a dryness, a dry contempt.
Night was what destroyed the legions;
Waterclocks drowned the hafted eagles.
Science and law are the errors of empire;
The barbarians were never the enemy.

The enemy does not fight, but dances.
Oh wind.
As each Etruscan knew.
At Tarquinia such
Greenness combs the cool brown earth;
Even a painted dog brings tears.

When I remember all my age,
When I remember all we wanted,
When the wind moves as now it moves
We live and I touch your sleeping hair.

At a Country-House Hotel

The air is sad, but then we laugh,
Sitting apart on the dry grey lawn . . .
Three from the other world, while
A woman from this one aimlessly wanders,
Widowed eyes on the grass between trees,
Gracious and ancient Berkshire trees,
And another sits reading a genteel novel.
These and the colonel with his wife
Are all.

It has come to this, this world
Once many-voiced and green with order;
The meadows, wells, the flowery walks,
The cottages and grovy parkland, the
Splendour, peace, and sage injustice.

This.
Silence.
The colonel comes from the kitchen door,
Walking obliquely with lowered eyes.

History is this rictus,
This rictus on the colonel's face
As he clears away our tea-things
Praying to God we've left no tip.

At Ostia

The girl in the almonds,
The orchard of barriers, soft green husks.
I stare through a doorway,
Stone eyes and quick eyes.
Cry of cicadas, panting lizard.
She is in shadow, I am in shadow,
Fringe upon fringe of airless leaves.

You are here, she says, you are here.
Listen, listen, do not move.
All these histories I have been waiting
And you did not come.
Over the tesserae slanting sun.
Her slanting eyes: I tease old men
But you may undress me.

In sunlight, shadow, luminous silence.
Fall of clothes; white skin is cool.
Love is the underside of leaves.
Is silence, silence, shifting shadow.

At the foot of the wall.

So long,
So long,
Why did you have to wait so long?

I Cannot See Her Face

I cannot see her face and
I cannot see the house's face
the year is gone yea exit all
the circumstance that mattered then

and she is nothing but that she
nameless beside me through her trees
time past that will not pass
tall fouroclock sunlight leafing

the lawn the Devon combe we walk
forever discovering there there
'here are my cyclamens' hitting
pink clusters perfect heads

why this
dead feet among the cyclamens
why this

Le Voyeur Vu

careless rain careless rain
drifts down across the midnight gardens
where opposite I watch one light
one window live above the trees

there Atropos with undrawn curtains
naked light undresses
in my dark Zeiss eyes and
stands five seconds in my sight

it is not sex that careless yawn
the upraised arms the small bare breasts
it is not what the textbooks say
but life: she is imagination

new-bodied in a nakedness
made real across the reason's void
all that I have not done all
I shall try to do in vain

the torment of the known unknown
the tense few seconds of the truth
before that casual stretching of an arm
then darkness and the long night's rain

A Tree in the Suburbs

I see them in their orange hosts,
Frail phalanx of the nearly dead.
They hang there in the window's eye
Like very ancient votive dolls
Whose meanings learned men dispute.
Trite yet tragic seem their falls –
That slip, that twirl, that touch
And swirl – and then oblivion,
The sodden grass. Meanwhile indoors
We find we have no contacts left,
No rites, no gods, no open lines.
And every winter things get worse.

The Rain Took the Road This Winter

My ancestors are anonyms –
In how many village graves are
bones, are dust, are voids
beneath unlettered stones.

None of them, it seems, achieved
a monument of act or speech,
or lives in anything
a living sense could reach.

A scatter of peasants, I would say,
of brute begetters,
who never did much bad or good
or got in history's way.

Were farriers, perhaps,
or shepherds in remoter combes,
or Georgian town-labourers
crimped in their tenemental rooms,

and later were solemn men with whiskers,
women with staid Victorian wombs,
but still trudging onward sending
a son or girl through death,

a living stem that stops in me:
this stopping of their blood in me
this brink, this ending of their hope
I think they do not understand.

Twice from a window in my heart
I have heard gatherings
and seen mysterious faces stand
grim witness to the house's hurt.

Dunnocks, Wrens

Dunnoks, wrens, small brown birds:
out of the interstices!
Out, out, and let my walls
lie in their long corruption.

John Clare

First violets by the west field wall:
Not all in vain, not all the vile
Misunderstandings of little men
Made blind by a quickset accent,
A prickly self-esteem, an ignorance
Of commas, colons . . . you were no
Orthographer. But still you knew
Ten thousand of their city minds
Could not begin to see you clear.
Your eyes, your tongue, your green
Fertility and voice.

Your eyes, not mine; your heart,
Not mine; your calloused hands,
Not mine. Eternally to you,
These violets by the west field wall.

You also broke the land too soon;
And made the rest seem all too late.

Parus Major

Springspeaker, syrinx in the green,
You bird a meanness killed,
Ounce tuft of broken wings;
The male is in the lilac,
Silent, silent, silent.

The debt. If
Sadness in one bird
What vast new payments
Lay proved to be paid.

Collecting Firewood

Fragments of canopy, fallen perches
Once full of sap and the insects' drone,
Of travertine leaves in the August sun:
I do not care, using you, calling you
Good or bad by dryness, wetness,
Whatever brief flame you can provide.

Then seeing my work as what it will be,
Sticks some cold new eye collects –
For this we die? – I throw
This perfect burning one away
To live a slower death than these:
These blended ashes in the hearth,
Illegible poets in last night's fire.

Nilmanet: Nocturne

Yek cries the magpie. The secret porpoise
rolls.
All is by opposites.
The apple's dark arms in the silver sea.

Night is a net
of many-meshed owls.
Hoot my mystery, mystery; their
silences loom meanings.
Assaults the land, roars on the Cobb.
Yaps, runs through the back lane
yapping at light, anxious, yapping.
First wren rips the dreaming shroud.

Once
centaury, gentian, star red the cropped grass.
The jewels went then the vermin went.
Now scrub, bracken, broken owls.
Dawn: all is by opposites.

Linnets

You absurdities. You antedaters
of Schoenberg, Stravinsky, how
dare you never sing the same song
twice?
Twitterers,
twizzlers of broken notes.
Yet for that divine exception
lodged in your dice-ridden throats:
that exquisite struck harp Tu
Fu once called
Wind in the Seven Pines
you are forgiven.

Aeshna Cyanea

It preys; it preys, uniquely hunts and preys
intenter than its paler human homonym
mutter of monks and saints mere frightened mouths
no shadow of stop chasing each sunlit hour

pure perfect it intensely is what it is
pure purpose plan pure honed design
its ultra-human need for gnats on gnats
no ego blinds, no pointless care for *tu*

it preys, patrols, just intent upon its flicker-cruise
two or three feet from the sunwarmed cobbles
razor-keen eyes whose myriad facets
whose sawtoothed mandibles poise and rake

so slim so beautiful so darting quick
so much here now but never quite where next
nothing could ever predict such cunning flight
mind-pure machine that bans the preordained

it might be human if it had a heart
I know I fell in love with it alone
I know it also lacks the simplest soul
and common sense would sooner kiss a stone

Aeshna cyanea is a brightly coloured species of Hawker Dragonfly. [Editor]

Accipiter

slit

the hurtle
the tilt and swathe

slit

the wings shut
leaning
hurtling
rickneck

slit

sliced second
gone before it came

At the bottom of Belmont, gardening by the bamboos: a sparrow-hawk. [John Fowles]

In New Jersey

For you I propose the most banal
of lives. You will grow uglier,
sillier, die and dissolve for ever.

You, tress of silk in the trees' darkness.
The river's dark ice. Your face
not to be seen, only the hair
in the frozen shadows.

Lunch at Jean Shrimpton's

Green fern in the window, green fern
beneath mirror with Mexican words;
some souvenir, I suppose.

The maidenhair looks dry. Its sill
has too much sun, would better suit
a greenhouse rose.

Some silly thing is said. In such
a place to disagree would be absurd;
I scratch my nose

and smile. The fern and mirror in the sun
sing something deep, most definitely
not meant for prose.

A marriage in them speaks to me, a
rightness in the frame, a harmony
of mood and pose

that sets them subtler than they seem
and slowly fills the room with cer-
tain quidproquos

only a traitor could pursue. Who knows
what unmapped other worlds there are
inside those

dull duets of love we fear to end?
What trigons of the heart and nerves?
But nothing shows.

Ces nymphes, je les veux perpétuer –
Shrimpton, giraffe with the angel's face,
and you, old faundoze

of my brain, too shrewd to mind
or believe in any seed I plant
until it grows.

Where Will It End?

What solids, structure, sure event!
This Victorian garden. It had always
A century in hand. Under the cedars.
And over the lawns beyond the lake
Bent labourers, sickles, small children
In blue with pale pink pinafores,
Prim and established, gently apart.

Turning to Henry, she smiled. Is not
Eternity that distant gardener
Crossing the lawn, bearing a tray
Of preferred pelargoniums? Such
Peace in milky, shadowed faces.

No harbingers, no threat or stress,
No children charred in the acrid smoke.
It happens still, dense and serene,
The harvesters in the hay's green mist.
While Henry stands, dundrearied, grave.

And now it's old. Yours. Junk
In the attic, dark canvas without a frame
Left by a relative no one remembers.
Could Henry and she have dreamt how warped?
How full of rents, how thin now on the void?

Strindberg

Among the pines. The sun at that angle
Light fires the turned, transparent page.
See how the old man stares through words,
Vain words, at the wordless light below.
Airs from the paling sea below: frail air
And evening. Those rheuming eyes,
Uncertain as the seeds of next year's spring.
They see nothing now. How veined the lids.
Vanilla, vanilla in her long-dead hair.
And Nurse comes silently, over the needles.

From an Unknown Planet

It was sitting in a lounge
and waiting for a flight we knew
would not be called. It didn't
matter.

We never knew the destination
and almost certainly it would have been
too late when we got there. We'd
have gone home, but home was sold,
stock and lock. Not for much,
it started cracking long before.
For the first time in our lives
we had just what we stood up in.
Actually we were sitting down.
Quite comfortable. Quite warm.
It didn't matter.

Quiet in the airport, nice quiet
groups. We found ways to amuse
ourselves. There were amply
the usual facilities.

You could say it had got too big.
Beyond one man, one nation,
beyond the species. A sad lack
of the obvious. The last clear tyrant
was much regretted, especially
by all who had hated him.

It was all on television, all
factors no one could have foreseen
and processes that were irreversible.
What could one do but watch?

There was a terrible shortage
of ignorance. Everyone knew.

The flatness won. In art
the cleverest explored the stalest.
Some blamed it on that.

Two men stood on our moon. Two
thousand million watched them.
It was a great achievement,
a good night's viewing.

More passengers arrived. Some
of the airline people apologised.
It was an effort sometimes
not to get up and speak. One
or two of the unbalanced screamed.
That also made good viewing.
One sat down again and watched.

It was like a vacuum. It was
waiting for mother to come
and set things right, knowing
she was dead and waiting for her
to come. A comfortably childish
impossibility. Nothing happened, and
waiting usurped the heart of things.
Once it had been tears.

The end, it is agreed, is near.
We regret hardly at all that
technical problems will prevent
the usual coverage and analysis.

Farewell. Be warned. Watch less.

At Belmont

1

You sit
watching
tennis
sunlit on television

dreaming of death
your own particular
death.
Creating a myth

why are you so?
Why in love with
shadows
darkness
and
endless
total blackness

why?
at this
summerlifetime
why

2

How many years since the loft
was used? A hundred years.
A hundred years this dusk
since the loft was used.

The empty stairs, the stone-grey light
silent above and shadowed below.
The empty top of the empty stairs
standing, waiting, staring down.

At the top of the stable stairs
stand eyes; not visible,
a death not death, not dead at all.
Terror. Some more familiar ghost

I could have dealt with.
But now this, my own death
standing, spaceless, peaceless,
implacably absent till I die.

Crabbing

The sun just risen, the moon still high,
And nothing but the morning's birds,
The gulls, the redshanks, razorbills
Beneath the pale young summer sky –

These birds, the windless air and sea:
Quicky, his mate, my nephew and I
Chug westward to the wooded shore
In outward peace and honesty.

We stop and start and slowly haul
The wicker pots. Upward they float
Ribbed from the sea's translucent depths.
Hove on the deck the brown crabs crawl

Each osier cell. Then Quicky's skill:
Catching them neatly through the mouth,
The massive claws bent back just so,
He nicks and cuts. They soon lie still,

Baffled by all this light and death,
Ligaments severed, pincers vain.
I watch my nephew's knife-fixed stare,
His six-years-old of bated breath

As each spiked monster joins the rest.
He may relive them in his dreams,
As I did once, and wake one night
To face his sanity's first test

As scuttling horrors throng his bed.
I dreamt this many times when young:
That I was drowned, the world was drowned,
Only my flesh and the crabs not dead.

I touch his hair, but not for that.
I think how he, when he is old,
Will make a better judgement throne
Of this benched gunwale where he sat,

Since time must teach him that this dawn
Held something that we hid from him:
How his had been a shadowed year
In which no lucky child was born.

He must remember us with rage,
We three men on a dying sea
Who saw the oil and slicks of scum,
All the foul poison of their age

Filmed out around them like pus,
Yet told him why the crabs got caught
Was out of stupid greed for bait.
We said they hadn't brains, like us.

Today he nods, and takes our word –
But what will he do when he looks back
And sees how cancerous-blind we were,
How sick, how viciously absurd?

Greed never trapped us in its cage.
We never sat and watched time haul
Earth onward to its stifled end.
He *must* remember us with rage.

Horror Movie

That photograph when I was four:
The small boy with his first toy bat.
My father is the foreground blur,
My mother wears the Twenties' hat.

Suburban cricket on the lawn:
First rule of life, eye on the ball.
The rebel in my Cornish heart
Has long since analysed it all.

So what remains? To take it down
From the old heart-wall where it hangs
And add the thing the camera missed:
The pair of comic vampire's fangs.

Statues in the Garden

The wicked women in the cold
Bare thighs, bare breasts.
Their plaster-plastic bodies
Seem almost to scream;
Oh God, for Jesus' sake warm us
Though we seem so far from flesh.

Not an Owl

Not an owl on the bough, after all;
but a patch of grey light forcing
through fir. A light-bird,
a bird-light. Retinal phantom.
Or poem to my shortening sight.

In the Middleyard

'Middleyard' is an Anglo-Saxon word meaning 'this world'.

Always the waves, their hiss and anger
Sexed to the sexed, though not to all.
God knows there are some distances
That must be kept; one must stay free,
Be many-minded, not just the selfish me.
If I were it, I'd stay above,
For this is best. If you must look, look down,
Though not to despise, but just to plumb.
Pin it you can't, it won't be one;
They live beyond all white imaginings of wait,
Of manyness, of space and change, of clicking time.

I feel Lyme calm today, October mild, and
Through my dim and clouded eyes, my computation
Of its is, the itness that it gains through me,
These three small girls infuse the sea.
They must touch nine. Their skinny costumes,
Shrieks and games, those ancient games,
Their gravities and grace . . .

Do airs and ripples twitch its mind?
My Greece, two thousand years or more ago
And now, Lolitas making love to liquid,
These screaming muses in the water:
Kilvert smiles and Carroll too; the other Charles,
He of the orchid and the worm, ignores.
                                        Some say
It is arachnoid, central, countless tipped
To sense each dark vibration of a chord,
Each Melusine and bearded monster…
Not me.

Like it, unfanged, I simply wait and watch
And am the empty soul. Lost in blue infinities
For one moment I sense the cosmos whole.

Washing in Nea Psychiko

Sometimes it seems there's no such thing.
Time lies, it simply doesn't move at all
Distilling each to all forever,
All being to one, all one in being,
As in these curtains, licked by light
And teased by snakes. Such flip and flap,
But no! Athanatos, it is my I alone
That speaks, not yours or any other.
You brew me among your muttering souls,
Your hands range washing down the rock-strewn shore
While dark Odysseus, nearly blind, limps bleakly past
Not seeing the marble gleams of light
Through each small second's two-tongued door.

The Posh Hospital Poems

Written in hospital during illness, 1994

1. Peccari: So Much Worse Than Bones

So much worse than bones, than burst intestines
Black and livid flesh, than torture's weals, this constant
Snow of care, Sarah, Circe, Sushila and Dianne,
All so kind that you forget. Surely at last you'll see
And now be warmer in return, show more concern;
Yet somehow nothing thaws, stays paperwhite
(You've never time, think those in need must be the same)
Pure crystals of the frozen will, so far far worse
Than all the jagged scars and shit; Rwanda,
Bosnia, that bolgered gunge of endless hell.

When did all the dinosaurs die, I clean forget
Though I've loved Socrates, the Bible and Candide.
My friends, at heart I'm ice, a haunted floe
Not hearing all I should, nor acting all I know.

2. On reading The Oxford Book of Schooldays

How can I bear them all, when I read this –
The once head boy, and captain of cricket too?
For five long years they drilled their way
Sapping both soul and mind, those bent small boys in tears;
But then, all their Gestapo work and beating done,
Of course we did our best to kill the Hun –
Despite the foulness their creed spread . . . which made us one.
Perhaps the cricket was the worst, to believe
All thought, all politics, all social truth
Could be compressed to one red ball
And worshipped like a god; and then that that was all.

3. The Moguls

Sweet, drifting through Bahr, Himayun, Akbar, Jehangir, Shakjahna,
Knowing they're gone, yet ring sharp bells; aesthetes all,
Both poets and peasants, precious brutes, and paradigms
Of all excess; Mongols mad to be themselves,
Quite sacrosanct from all forbidden;
Preferring garden tents to walls,
Tough as the camels they would not ride,
Proud of their towers of trunkless heads
Often half-doped, full-pissed or blotto,
But oh such splendid shahs of shape and colour,
So neat in *jama* and *jharaokha*, so owning all!
Say I could be the ruler of Sawar, Raj Singh,
Ensconced among my sages, servants, trees and birds . . .
You can keep that dull old thing of Kublai Khan's.

4. Why Do We Always Know

Why do we always know they're luckier?
That unknown car outside the door
Their leaving alone, that glimpsed embrace
That hint they're going to another place
Or meeting someone you've not met
Some joy that you will never get.

5. Muslins

Always by glimpses, thinnest seeps, some slit
Of cloth suggesting sin inside the web
Which wafts these long-swathed hints of sari
Swanned always in transparent heat; whose shadows stain
Each jalousie, each frustration, in the grille . . .
The whisperings, mutterings, muffled yelps!
So princed and paired, kohl-eyed and curled,
We think of how the moguls' wasted seed
Was lost by lust and conned by each sweet suck
Of hookahed hemp. Empires of myths,
Not entities, half seen and never truly understood . . .
Like you, my love, half bare yet muslined in my mind,
Light-borne in India, the slim small dream
That drifts behind this pale, see-through, half-serious theme.

6. Forks

So many things one cannot, must not say.
It is absurd, the hedging day on day, to funk the brink
One cannot cross. Sometimes it seems you're wise;
Sometimes, in view of what the other time
Might once have brought, unbearable loss.
Or no, one jumps a word, the movement
Of a hand or just some undressed thought,
And then you're stuck; wrapped blind inside a black, black world
That endless evil web in which all choosing flies are caught.

7. Beneath the Blue

for Circe

I can hardly speak, and you not well; so eyes
Alone, swift touch of hands between the bars
The black, black bars, so many unsure words.
There is asymmetry in all we are, our times
As unmatched as our tongues, two psyches lost in night.
I know you're just a myth, we met by chance.
While I'm grotesque, a world from any Ulysses
Yet tell me why, if we first met whole ages past
It still seems yesterday and poems tremble
At each breath. I tread the dark Aegean shore
And walk towards that haunting green inside
Your shadowed eyes. Why do such ancient pasts
Seem almost now? What makes us crave our former parts?
What strange green vine still binds our hearts?

Behind and Behind

It seems, with so much death noosed tight around
I do not like the being tied;
Like some sly lurcher bored with hunting
Prefer the trees, the slinking there to hide

Why I Cried at Porto Rafti

Not both. Your blue idyllic land . . .
And you as well. Dear God, not both.
Too much, it's truly more than I can bear.

I am so very ill, sweet nurse.
You've no idea how soon I'd die
If your green eyes were never there.

There Is No God

There is no God.
There is nothing
other.
There is only
only all we apprehend.

I sit on my back patio surrounded
by friends. I call them
friends, but they are not
                                        known.

TRANSLATIONS/VERSIONS

Aristophanes

Editor's Note: In Fowles's 1982 essay, *The Falklands and a Death Foretold*, he speaks with outrage of 'the monster' that is war, and how easily it can be resurrected through word and image. Aristophanes's highly political play *Peace* (421 BC) was produced just before the close of the ten-year Peloponnesian war. Fowles chose to translate the Chorus's celebrated parabasis, sung during the peace festivities as both recollection and anticipation of ordinary times. 'Thratta' was a standard name for a slave-girl.

Peace

It's good, so good to be free of the helmet,
to be free of stale cheese and dry onions.
Give me a ring of old friends round a fire,
a fire of dry logs cut in the dog-days,
and the wine passing round the flames.
Then fry me a plate of chick-peas, roast me
a few beechnuts and let me have a go at Thratta
while her mistress takes her bath.

Or is there anything to compare with rain,
the pleasure rain gives when the seeds are sown?
When a neighbour comes in and says
What's to do today, old friend?
To which I reply, The sky works for us.
I feel like a drink. Mistress! Cook
us a dish of beans and wheat, and show us
your figs. Tell Syra to call Manes
back from the fields. It's no good pruning
the vines today, and the ground's too wet
to turn. And then my friend says to me –
I'll just get someone to run back home
to fetch a thrush and a couple of finches.

I think there's some curdled milk as well,
and four pieces of hare, that is if the cat
didn't snitch his share last night –
I heard a devil of a row in the kitchen.
Give one bit to father, lad, and bring us
the other three. Ask old Eschinades
for some myrtle twigs, and call out on your way
to Charinades – tell him to come along
and have a drink, since the sky works for us
and does the crops good.

And is there anything to compare with summer,
when the cicada's strong in his friendly racket,
and you walk round your Lemnos vines
to see how the grapes are coming on –
because they ripen early, that sort –
and you see how the figs are getting fat,
and when they are ripe, you stuff them
in your mouth, and savour them, and cry –
such hours as these are worth the living!
And back home one brews oneself a drink
and flavours it with thyme – O that's the season
for getting fat . . .

Martial

Editor's Note: In the draft of an undated letter to a BBC producer, Fowles suggested 'doing a programme' on the epigrams of Martial (c.40–c.104 AD), pointing out that they 'were (unlike a lot of poetry!) deliberately written to entertain, and also to be publicly uttered'. He hoped for a reader whose voice was 'sufficiently acid'. He explained – and this provides an insight into all his various translations – that he has tried 'to make them as unarchaic as possible . . . [and] to preserve the "line" and sting of each epigram. They are free translations, but almost all of the freedom lies in the omission of mythological or geographical reference which could hardly mean much to the non-specialised listeners.' This is a very small selection from some 130 examples.

1.39

You recite my poems.
But you recite so badly
They begin to be yours.

1.72

Six glasses for Naevia,
Seven for Justina,
Five for Lycas, four
For Lydea, Ida, three.
I count each girl in the wine poured.
None comes
But Sleep will sleep with me.

1.74

No one would have touched your wife
When she was there for the touching;
Now you have people to guard her,
And the gigolos swarm at your door.

Brilliant!

12.41

You are afraid I might write an epigram
About you. You are also longing
To find that your fear is justified.
But both fear and longing are in vain.
Lions kill bulls, not butterflies.
Find some drunken brother rhymer
If you want to be celebrated.
Let him scrawl charcoal or coarse chalk lines about you
In a public lavatory.

Your head is not for my branding.

1.41

You who pull such a face
And read this so unwillingly,
You envy everybody; but
Nobody envies you.

7.25

Always the most sweet and elegant epigrams.
Whiter than white-enamelled skin,
So free of salt, so free of acid.
And you expect them to be read!

One doesn't eat food without condiments.
One doesn't like faces that never smile.
Give quinces in honey to children;
But give me the tang of a Chian fig.

Catullus

Editor's Note: Catullus (died c. 54 BC) was a particular favourite of Fowles's, who relished the lyric poet's emotional sincerity and caustic bawdiness. A scribble at the bottom of one of the typescript pages notes that 'the poets (Catullus, Juvenal, Martial) . . . still love the idea of the Greek ephebe-man relationship. That is, they love any spontaneous love; and loathe any professional fabricator of sex.'

XIII Fabullus

Fabullus a meal to remember
come and have it with me soon

only please bring it
bring it and bring
a beddable trollop
wine wit and laughter

you won't regret it
but I'm broke
purse of cobwebs

I'll give you love
love neat
or anything nicer

I'll give you the scent
the sex-gods gave my girl
when you smell it
you'll pray to be nothing
but nose
Fabullus
nothing but nose

LVI

Cato you'll like this
absurd you'll laugh
I know you like me so laugh
it's absurd ridiculous
I caught a little boy
wiggling his thighs like a girl
so
erect man that I am
for propriety's sake
I punished him stiffly

II Lesbia

sparrow
thing she loves
plays with
holds between her breasts
gives her first finger to
teasingly
you
sharp pecker

when the whim takes her
at the times she bright
one I love
cannot love
you ease her pain

if I could play with you
to ease my pain

XXXI *paene insularum, Sirmio, insularum*

almost-island island of islands
Sirmio my Sirmio
I come again so light in heart
still feeling there
there in the dull Bithynian scrub
not here safe

feeling so free of cares
mind free
home again here
home from the endless travelling
here on the bed so often longed for
this is what all the stress was for

I greet you my place
sing for my homecoming
lovely loved place loved lake
be happy now
all happiness home for me

Philostratus

Editor's Note: Flavius Philostratus was a Greek sophist of the Roman period who died c. 245 AD. Ben Jonson drew on one of Philostratus's erotic *Epistolae* for 'Drink to Me Only with Thine Eyes'.

Love Letters

To Chariton

You think we shall remember
Every single word you've said –
A nonentity now you are living,
But immortal once you are dead.

To Athenodorus

They say it is magic, your living
in Corinth and loving a boy
who lives in Ionia, a boy
you've simply heard about.
Through the eyes love enters mind;
but the mind can see nothing,
and not be blind.

Alciphron

Editor's Note: The Greek philosopher Alciphron lived probably in the second century AD. His exquisite letters are fictions penned by various classes of people; they were first published in full in 1715.

Letters

1.20, Eusagenus to Limenarchus

That lad from Lesbos – the lookout!
He'd better!
Because he saw the water a bit dark
he called us a shoal of tunny.
So we paid out the seine,
we laid the seine around the bay,
and started hauling.
Sure enough, it was heavy,
no ordinary catch.
So we cried to some people nearby
and promised them part of the haul
if they helped. Which they did –
the whole afternoon.
Near dusk, we had it.

A fine big camel, rotten with worms.
It doesn't make me laugh;
I'm telling you this
to prove fate is against me.

2.24, Gemellus to Salaconis

So you make fun of me, Salaconis.
There wasn't any fuss from you
or your mother
when I first spotted you
in that lame tailor's shop
and carried you off.
I set you up here,
treating you like a bride
with a big dowry on her head.
But now, you little tart, you've got
grand ideas and you giggle.
You make fun of me.

You make fun of me, and you giggle.

I'll make you roast barley out on the farm!
I'll teach you the hard way
not to make fun of your lover and master.
Jupiter, I'll teach you who's master!

2.25, Salaconis to Gemelus

Anything, anything,
but I can't sleep with you.
I wasn't hiding out in the scrub
last night.
I was under the kneading-trough.

I am going to hang myself,
So I can say what I like.
I loathe you.

I loathe your hairy fox-foul body
as I loathe your filthy mouth
with its deep-throat reek.

You are vile. I wish you a vile death.
Go and screw an old ratbag
With only one tooth and eczema!

2.34, Pratinus to Megaloteles

What a bore, what a bore he was –
that soldier arriving late one afternoon,
picking on us for a billet,
and talking, talking, talking . . .
that military vocabulary!
Squads and phalanxes, catapults,
flamethrowers, mantelets . . . ugh!
Then how he had routed a Thracian tribe
by catching their chief in the eye
with a javelin sling. And how he had run
an Armenian through with a pike,
and the prisoners he'd taken
and the girls he'd got as reward
for his splendid conduct . . .

to shut him up,
I gave him wine, a big bowlful, another,
another, a stronger, another
and others . . .
but still his tongue went marching on.

From the Chinese

Editor's Note: The following poets are among the most celebrated of the 'golden' Tang Dynasty (618–907). Fowles's versions are relatively free.

Li Po

There is moonlight on my bed,
There is frost upon the ground.
Staring at the moon, I think
There must be frost upon the ground.
Then turn, remembering home.

Wang Ch'ang-Ling

The river we ford and the wind are cold.
The horses are watered. Over the plain
The autumn sun has not quite set.
In the last light we see Kansu,
Great walls where once great wars
Were fought, and heroes made.
Around us, past and present are one.
Whitely among the untrammelled weeds
Lie bones.

Li Shang-Yin

When shall I come home again?
Here in the hills the evening rains
Swell out the autumn pools.
How can I ever tell you
When we shall sit again in the western window,
Snuffing candles and talking of how
Here in the hills the evening rains
Swelled out the autumn pools?

From the Japanese

Editor's Note: The *Man'yoshu* was compiled by Yakamochi, who died in 785. It is the oldest and finest anthology of Japanese poetry, and includes poems dating back to at least the fifth century. Its chief poets, apart from Yakamochi himself, are Akahito and Hitomaro; others chosen by Fowles in his considerable selection (and presented here) include Princess Oku, the Lady of Sakanoye, the priest Hakutsu and Kunimoto. The prevailing form is the five-line tanka, two lines longer than the haiku.

Now it is autumn
how will you cross the mountain
          so hard to cross
when we were still together

I am dying of love
when she walks past my door
          she says
          die!

let them multiply,
          the words of men
like the grass on the summer uplands
    so long as she and I
    lie hand in hand

though I am on an official journey
and have candle-light this evening
    perhaps she is in the dark
          thinking of me

his dress is thin
o Sao wind blow soft
    till he comes

they are gone hunting
        the gallant husbands
along the clean sands
        trail
the red petticoats of their wives

the face of the pine-tree
    by my house
        is like the face of a man
    who died long ago

I saw you two days ago,
    I saw you yesterday,
        and now
    o you
desirable-to-see-tomorrow-too

in my dream
he promised to come
    when evening comes
I will open my door,
and wait

sad
those meetings in dreams
        when one wakes up alarmed
        stretches out the hand
    to touch the no-one there

I wanted to see you but
        I pretended
    to examine the state of the bamboo fence

our love who can know it
　　this delicate pillow
if anything can know it

　　　　the moon
　　over the rushes
　　　　of Imami moor
　　how could we make love indoors

That insect in the pines
whose bored cry echoes
through the autumn night;
who was it expecting?

The cry among the reeds;
remembering something
it wanted to forget.

The white clouds driven by the wind
split on the hill-top.
Is your heart quite worthless?

Like the winter river,
frozen over white ice.
But love underneath.

Like a letter in faint ink,
the geese returning in the mist.

The image of the moon in water;
cupped here in my hand,
I see my life.

What is life?
White wake of a ship
that left at dawn.

Is it sad for me alone?
Or was it sad
from the very beginning?

Here in the plain of reeds
beside the abandoned house
the cherry blossom falls,
and has no sorrow.

If he comes, he
I have waited for so long,
what shall I do?
He will want to tread
on the snow in the garden.

The falling of the leaves
makes it difficult to tell
the nights with a little rain
from the nights with no rain.

Dawn is sad.
The trembling sunrise.
The helping each other to dress.

That it was the road one takes,
I knew.
But yesterday I never thought
it would be today.

Never forgotten; not even
for a flash of lightning,
on a field of autumn corn.

La Fontaine

Editor's Note: The following are drawn from Jean de la Fontaine's licentious *Contes* (1664–74), less familiar than his renowned *Fables.*

There was a man

There was a man who went to war
And stayed away a year or more.
Back home at last a knight he came
But found his home was not the same.
He hardly knew his shy young wife
Who now was gay and full of life;
Who now had friends he did not know,
Young men who called themselves her beaux.

'So this is how things come about?
Am I deceived? I must find out.'
He thought and thought, and found a way.
As a priest he dressed one day
And went to where his wife confessed.
What happened then is easily guessed.
The trollop came, demurely knelt;
Nothing suspected, nothing felt.
Inside the box her husband sat;
Innocent mouse, and waiting cat.
The sins she told at first were small
But these alas were far from all,
And soon she had to change her key.

'Father, I have sinned,' said she,
'A gentleman, a priest, a knight
Have all seemed pleasant to my sight
And all have slipped into my bed . . .'

Many another she would have said
If then her husband had not cried –
'O faithless woman! Faithless bride!
You do not know who is inside!'
The wife was quick, hid all surprise.
'Husband, I saw through your disguise.
You were gentleman, then a knight,
And now a priest. Is that not right?'

'Praise God,' he cried. 'Then I'm not horned!'
'Praise God,' she thought, 'that I was warned.'

Once a village girl

Once a village girl called Jane
Broke a jug beside a lane.
She was just a dairy-maid
And of her mistress much afraid.
What to do she did not know,
She feared her cruel mistress so.
The more she thought, the more she cried;
At last elected suicide.
A handsome lad who happened by
Asked her how she came to cry,
And when he heard what she designed
Tried hard to make her change her mind.
But on her death she was resolved.
From his scruples thus absolved
He asked a favour – if die she must
She might the act to him entrust.
Poor Jane agreed. He threw her down
And tumbled up her little gown
And stabbed her with a certain knife
Good husbands give a willing wife.
Jane rolled her eyes and softly groaned,
Jane cried aloud and strangely moaned.
Again and again he gave her death
Until he was quite out of breath.
'O thank you, thank you, sir,' she said,
'I feel much better now I'm dead.
And if one always dies this way,
I'll break a new jug every day.'

A young and pretty maid

A young and pretty maid she was
And what she was she did not hide.
The mother came at dawn that day
Her son would take his bride away;
In his house she found the son
And the charming maid as one.
'Shame on you, my boy!' she cried.
'Have you not a virgin bride?'
'O mother, mother, do be calm.
What I do will cause no harm
For Alison is but the stone
To whom I give my blade to hone.'

Once there was a little nun

Once there was a little nun,
For once a most improper one;
She had a lover in the town
And when they met she did not frown;
But meet in private they could not
And most unhappy was their lot.
But little nuns are never slow;
A sempstress to her cell did go,
At least a sempstress by the frock.
To work in peace they turned the lock,
But what they did there is no knowing;
No doubt they passed the day in sewing.
Night came; the sempstress had to go –
A pity, when one likes to sew.
'Goodbye, dear sister! Sempstress, goodbye!
Till next time may dull hours fly!'
The nun went running to her vespers;
Was late; the chapel filled with whispers.
The abbess cried, 'So late? For shame!'
'Reverend mother, my sempstress came.'
'All day that woman stayed with you –
Had you so much work to do?'
'O reverend mother, more,' she sighed,
'The dear might work until she died
But never could she reach the end
Of all her needle needs to mend.'

There was a nun

There was a nun who had a child,
But then from being very wild
Became a saint. She prayed,
Fasted, never strayed.
Unlike her sisters whose confessions
Turned always into tedium sessions.
To them one day their abbess cried,
'Let your sister be your guide,
Forget the carnal world outside.'
To which at once the nun replied:
'But we shall all be saints as well –
When we have fallen as she fell.'

Afterword

First published as the Foreword to Fowles's Poems *(1973)*

If publication is not the business of poets, then even more surely it is not self-exegesis. But since this collection must, after the fact of my published novels, have something of the air of an autobiographical footnote, I should like to say briefly where poetry sits in my writing life.

The so-called 'crisis' of the modern novel has to do with its self-consciousness. The fault was always inherent in the form, since it is fundamentally a kind of game, an artifice that allows the writer to play hide-and-seek with the reader. In strict terms a novel is a hypothesis more or less ingeniously and persuasively presented – that is, first cousin to a lie. This uneasy consciousness of lying is why in the great majority of novels the novelist apes reality so assiduously; and is why giving the game away – making the lie, the fictitiousness of the process, explicit in the text – has become such a feature of the contemporary novel. Committed to invention, to people that never existed, to events that never happened, the novelist wants either to sound 'true' or to come clean.

Poetry proceeds by a reverse path: its superficial form may be highly artificial and *invraisemblable*, but its content is normally a good deal more revealing of the writer than prose fiction. The poem is saying what you are and feel, the novel is saying what invented characters might be and might feel. Only very naïve readers can suppose a novelist's invented personages and their opinions are reliable guides to his real self – that because Fanny Price represents Jane Austen's idea of the highest moral good, then meeting Jane Austen herself would have been like meeting Fanny. I have myself got a little tired of being taken for an all-wise millionaire on a remote Greek island.

Of course some poets wear masks (though much more for rhetorical than seriously deceitful reasons) and of course there is an autobiographical element in all novels. Nonetheless, I think there is a vital distinction. It is rather difficult to put one's private self into a novel; it is rather difficult to keep it out of a poem. A novelist is like an actor on stage, and his private self has to be subjugated to the public master of his novel's ceremonies. His primary audience is other people. A poet's is his or her own self.

This may, I think, partly explain why some writers are poets and others novelists – and why excellence in both forms is such a rare thing. I suspect most novelists are trying to camouflage a sense of personal inadequacy in the face of real life – a sentiment that is compounded in the act of creating fiction, the fabrication of literary lies, ingenious fantasies, to hide a fundamental psychological or sociological fault of personality. Some novelists – Hemingway is the classic instance – create a real-life as well as a literary *persona* in answer to this predicament. Most genuine poets have a much happier, or less queasy, relationship with their private selves. At least they do not live, like most novelists, in permanent flight from the mirror.

At any rate I have always found the writing of poetry, which I began before I attempted prose, an enormous relief from the constant play-acting of fiction. I never pick up a book of poems without thinking that it will have one advantage over most novels: I shall know the writer better at the end of it. I do not have to hope this is true of what follows.

John Fowles, 1972

Purgatory

I used to keep my poems in
a file called this:
I wonder why. This dull
and rainless winter
            morning
Dear Jean, now helped by Sarah,
types away

John Fowles (1926–2005) is widely regarded as one of the most innovative and important English novelists of the second half of the twentieth century. Born in Leigh-on-Sea, a small town on the Thames Estuary, he found his suburban childhood stiflingly conformist. For most of the Second World War he was a boarder at a boys' public school in Bedford, and in 1944 was called up for two-years' national service. He subsequently took a degree in French at Oxford, where he discovered and was influenced by such radical anti-authoritarian and anti-Establishment French existentialists as Jean-Paul Sartre and Albert Camus. Indeed, Fowles found himself as something of a Camusian rebel at war with convention.

After Oxford he taught first at Poitiers University in France, then on the Greek island of Spetsia for two years, before returning to London to work at St Godric's College until 1963. During the 1950s he began to write poetry and subsequently fiction, inspired especially by his experiences in Greece, but did not try to publish immediately. His first published novel, *The Collector* (1963), was a major critical as well as commercial success, and achieved bestseller status. This enabled him to abandon teaching and devote himself to full-time writing. The 1965 film version directed by William Wyler also proved to be very popular. In 1964 he brought out his first non-fiction book, *The Aristos*, a personal philosophical manifesto. This was followed by his magnum opus, *The Magus*, a highly original novel set in Greece on which he had been working for many years.

In 1965 he moved to Lyme Regis on the south-west coast, a town that featured in his next novel, *The French Lieutenant's Woman* (1969), a postmodernist take on Victorian fiction that also became a bestseller. The 1981 film version, with a screenplay by Harold Pinter, directed by Karel Reisz and starring Meryl Streep, was a triumphant success. Subsequent works of fiction are *The Ebony Tower* (1974), *Daniel Martin* (1977), *Mantissa* (1982) and *A Maggot* (1985). He also published a number of non-fiction books, but his only book of poetry, simply called *Poems*, came out in the USA (but not in the UK) in 1973.

Adam Thorpe is a novelist, critic, poet and playwright. He was born in Paris in 1956 and grew up in India, Cameroon and England. His first collection of poetry, *Mornings in the Baltic* (1988), was shortlisted for the 1988 Whitbread Poetry Award. His most recent books of poetry are *Birds with a Broken Wing* (2007), shortlisted for the Forward Prize, and *Voluntary* (2012), a Poetry Book Society Recommendation. Author of many works of fiction, his debut novel *Ulverton* won the Winifred Holtby Memorial Prize in 1992 and his reimagining of Robin Hood, *Hodd* (2009), was shortlisted for the Walter Scott Prize. His translation of Flaubert's *Madame Bovary* (2011) is published by Vintage.